Mel Bay Presents

Turkey in the STRAW
Bluegrass Songs for Children

traditional & original
songs by Phil Rosenthal

Cover design & inside artwork
by Suzanne Langlois

A recording of the music in this book is now available. The publisher strongly recommends the use of this recording along with the text to insure accuracy of interpretation and ease in learning.

IN CONJUNCTION WITH AMERICAN MELODY

Contents

Ain't Gonna Rain No More

Traditional

Verse 1:

Oh ___ what did the black-bird say to the crow, It ain't gon-na rain no more,

Ain't gon-na hail and it ain't gon-na snow, It ain't gon-na rain no more. Oh, it

Chorus:

ain't gon-na rain no mo-re no more, It ain't gon-na rain no more,

How in the heck can I wash my neck, When it ain't gon-na rain no more?

Guitar acc.

Last verse modulates to the key of F♯. To play along with the recording, put your capo on the second fret and play the regular chord.

AIN'T GONNA RAIN NO MORE

Verse 2:
    Bake those biscuits good and brown,
    It ain't gonna rain no more.
    Swing your partner 'round and 'round,
    It ain't gonna rain no more.

Chorus 1:
    Oh, it ain't gonna rain no more, no more,
    It ain't gonna rain no more,
    How in the heck can I wash my neck,
    When it ain't gonna rain no more?

Chorus 1:
    Oh, it ain't gonna rain no more, no more,
    It ain't gonna rain no more,
    How in the heck can I wash my neck,
    When it ain't gonna rain no more?

Chorus 2:
    It ain't gonna rain no more, no more,
    It ain't gonna rain no more,
    How do you suppose the old man knows,
    It ain't gonna rain no more?

Verse 1, Chorus 1, Chorus 2 (Key of F#)

Open Up the Window, Noah

Phil Rosenthal, based on traditional

OPEN UP THE WINDOW, NOAH

Verse 2:
> For forty long days it will be stormy and dark,
> Open up the window, let the dove fly in.
> So Noah, get ready, now build you an ark.
> Open up the window, let the dove fly in.

Chorus:

Verse 3:
> The water is rising, there's no time to lose,
> Open up the window, let the dove fly in.
> Go gather the creatures all in by twos.
> Open up the window, let the dove fly in.

Chorus:

Verse 1:
> The little bird flew to the window and mourned,
> Open up the window, let the dove fly in.
> Get ready, old Noah, there's coming a storm.
> Open up the window, let the dove fly in.

Chorus two times:

Snowy Day

by Phil Rosenthal

SNOWY DAY

Verse 3:
While the snowflakes fly, we'll stay warm and dry,
By the fireside this snowy day.

Verse 4:
Through the sky of white, I see geese in flight,
What a pretty sight, this snowy day.

Verse 5:
Dad comes from the barn, bringing in his arm
Wood to keep us warm, this snowy day.

Verse 6:
Icy windowpane, snowdrifts on the lane.
Nothing looks the same, this snowy day.

Verse 1:
Snowflakes falling down, covering the ground,
White fields all around, this snowy day.

Bingo

Traditional, with new lyrics by Phil Rosenthal

BINGO

Verse 2:
    Now every time he wanted him,
    He called him just the same-o.
    B-I-N-G-O, B-I-N-G-O, B-I-N-G-O, Bingo was his name-o.

Verse 3:
    You'd always see him chasing sticks,
    He loved to play that game-o.
    B-I-N-G-O, B-I-N-G-O, B-I-N-G-O, Bingo was his name-o.

Verse 4:
    He dropped that stick right at my feet,
    Every time I came-o.
    B-I-N-G-O, B-I-N-G-O, B-I-N-G-O, Bingo was his name-o.

Verse 5:
    Oh, Bingo loved to lick my hand,
    He was so very tame-o.
    B-I-N-G-O, B-I-N-G-O, B-I-N-G-O, Bingo was his name-o.

Verse 1:
    There was a farmer had a dog,
    And Bingo was his name-o.
    B-I-N-G-O, B-I-N-G-O, B-I-N-G-O, Bingo was his name-o.
    B-I-N-G-O, B-I-N-G-O, B-I-N-G-O, Bingo was his name-o.

Sailing in the Boat

Traditional, with new lyrics by Phil Rosenthal

Verse 1:

Sail - ing in the boat when the tide runs high, Sail - ing in the boat when the tide runs high, Sail - ing in the boat when the tide runs high, Wait - ing for the pret - ty girls to come by and by.

Verse 2:

Heave on the anchor and pull on the oar.
I see a pretty girl standing on the shore.
She is the maiden I adore.
I'll walk with her to her mama's door.

Verse 3:

She is a beauty so fresh and fair,
With sky blue eyes and curly hair,
Rosy cheeks, a dimple in her chin,
Sorry, young man, but you can't come in.

Verse 4:
There's a rose in the garden for you, young man,
A rose in the garden, pick it if you can.
Smells so sweet, and it looks so grand
But you better take care not to prick your hand.

Verse 5:
Be my partner, and dance all day.
I'll swing you around while the banjos play.
First to the right, then the other way,
And never you mind what the old folks say.

Verse 6:
Let's go down to the open sea,
Where the wind is humming a melody.
We'll float like a feather, light and free,
If you'll come sailing in the boat with me.

Verse 1:
Sailing in the boat when the tide runs high,
Sailing in the boat when the tide runs high,
Sailing in the boat when the tide runs high,
Waiting for the pretty girls to come by and by.

Riding in the Buggy

Traditional, with new lyrics by Phil Rosenthal

Verse 2:
Fare thee well, my little bitty Ann,
My little bitty Ann, my little bitty Ann,
Fare thee well, my little bitty Ann,
I must be on my way.

Verse 3:
Don't know when I'm coming back,
I'm coming back, I'm coming back,
Don't know when I'm coming back,
But I'll be back some day.

Chorus:

Verse 1:
Riding in the buggy, Miss Mary Jane,
Miss Mary Jane, Miss Mary Jane,
Riding in the buggy, Miss Mary Jane,
A long way from home.

Chorus:

Listen to the Bluegrass

Phil Rosenthal

Verse 1:

Lis - ten to the man -do - lin, don't you love that sound?

Don't you love the way the notes go___ run - ning all a - round?

Some are high, and some are low, and all of them are grand, That's

why we need a man-do - lin play - ing in our band.

Verse 5 modulates to the key of E. To play along with the recording, put your capo on the second fret and play the regular chords.

LISTEN TO THE BLUEGRASS

Verse 2:
   Listen to the old guitar play the melody.
   The notes are ringing sweet and low, and they sound good to me.
   Some are fast and some are slow, and all of them are grand,
   That's why I love to hear guitar playing in our band.

Verse 3:
   Listen to the banjo, doesn't it sound fine?
   I love to hear that banjo in this band of mine.
   It makes me want to tap my feet, don't you understand,
   That's why we need a banjo playing in our band.

Verse 4:
   Listen to the bass now, don't you love that sound?
   Don't you love the way the notes are all so fat and round?
   It gives our song a steady beat, don't you understand,
   That's why we need a bass fiddle playing in our band.

Verse 5:
   Listen to our bluegrass band, don't you love this sound?
   I think bluegrass music is the finest thing around.
   It makes me want to tap my feet, don't you understand,
   That's why I love to sing along with a bluegrass band.

19

Twinkle, Twinkle, Little Star

Traditional

20

TWINKLE, TWINKLE, LITTLE STAR

Chorus 1:
> When the blazing sun is gone,
> When he nothing shines upon,
> Then you show your little light,
> Twinkle, twinkle, all the night.

Verse 2:
> Hear the traveler in the dark,
> Thank you for your tiny spark.
> He could not see which way to go,
> If you did not twinkle so.

Chorus 2:
> In the dark blue sky you keep,
> And often through my curtains peep.
> For you never shut your eye,
> Till the sun is in the sky.

Verse 3:
> How your bright and tiny spark,
> Lights the traveler in the dark.
> Though I know not what you are,
> Twinkle, twinkle, little star.

Chorus 1:
> Twinkle, twinkle, little star,
> How I wonder what you are.
> Up above the world so high,
> Like a diamond in the sky.

Aiken Drum

AIKEN DRUM

Verse 2:
 His hair, it was spaghetti,
 Spaghetti, spaghetti.
 His hair it was spaghetti,
 And his name was Aiken Drum.

Chorus:

Verse 3:
 His nose, it was a carrot,
 A carrot, a carrot.
 His nose, it was a carrot,
 And his name was Aiken Drum.

Chorus:

Verse 4:
 His eyes, they were two raisins,
 Two raisins, two raisins.
 His eyes, they were two raisins,
 And his name was Aiken Drum.

Chorus:

Verse 5:
 His mouth, it was a tomato,
 A tomato, a tomato.
 His mouth, it was a tomato,
 And his name was Aiken Drum.

Chorus:

Verse 6:
 His head, it was a pumpkin pie,
 A pumpkin pie, a pumpkin pie.
 His head, it was a pumpkin pie,
 And his name was Aiken Drum.

Chorus:

Verse 7:
 Now wasn't he a yummy man,
 A yummy man, a yummy man?
 Wasn't he a yummy man,
 And his name was Aiken Drum.

Chorus:

Verse 1:
 There was a man lived in the moon,
 In the moon, in the moon.
 There was a man lived in the moon,
 And his name was Aiken Drum.

Little Liza Jane

Traditional

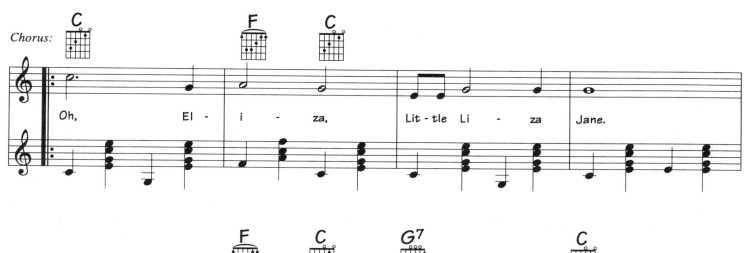

Oh, El - i - za, Lit - tle Li - za Jane.

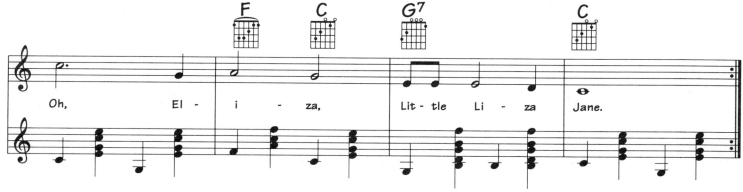

Oh, El - i - za, Lit - tle Li - za Jane.

Verse 3:
I'm going up on the mountain top,
Plant me a patch of cane.
I'm going to make molasses,
To sweeten Liza Jane.

Verse 4:
You go down that old fence road,
I'll go down the lane.
You can hug an old fence post,
I'll hug Liza Jane.

Chorus:

Verse 5:
Come along, sweet Liza Jane,
Come along with me.
We'll go up on the mountain top,
Some pleasures there to see.

(Repeat first verse)

Chorus:

Turkey in the Straw

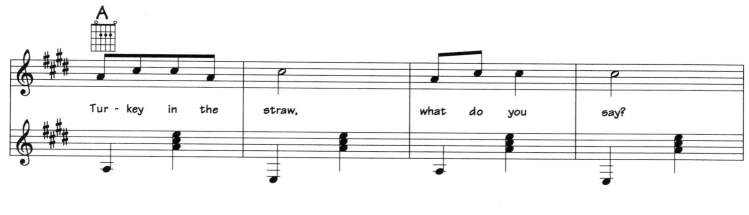

Tur - key in the straw, what do you say?

Funn - i - est thing___ I ev - er saw,

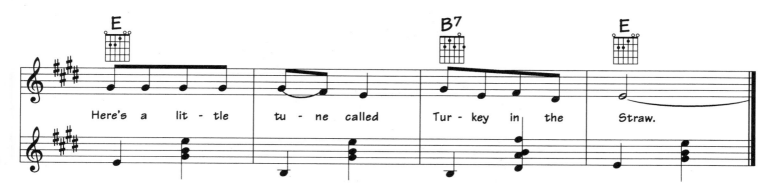

Here's a lit - tle tu - ne called Tur - key in the Straw.

Verse 2:
Well, I came to the river and I couldn't get across,
So I paid five dollars for an old blind horse.
He wouldn't go ahead and he wouldn't stand still,
He just went up and down like an old saw mill.

Chorus:

Verse 3:
Oh, I went out to milk, but I didn't know how,
I milked the goat instead of the cow.
A monkey sitting on a pile of straw,
Winking his eyes at his mother-in-law.

Chorus:

Verse 1:
As I was riding down the road,
With a two horse wagon and a four horse load,
I cracked my whip and the lead horse sprung,
And I said good-bye to the wagon tongue.

Chorus:
Turkey in the straw, turkey in the hay,
Turkey in the straw, what do you say?
Funniest thing I ever saw,
Here's a little tune called Turkey in the Straw.

(Repeat chorus)